"With this earthy and honest collection, Agnes Vojta shows us what it is to be an immigrant, removed from family by miles but not heart. She shares the familiar and walks us with her loved ones through small moments into grand revelations. "I was a stranger. Did not know/ the names of tree or bird./ Naming is knowing." Each poem is a naming of moments and observations, of memories and fears. Vojta's graceful writing holds us with delicate stark patience through her discoveries and losses into a collection we can return to with grateful reverence. "She whispers words/ that are missing/ in the dictionary,/ roars them in her rapids."

> - Jonie McIntire, Lucas County Ohio Poet Laureate (2022-2024); poetry editor of *Rust And Glass*; author of *Semidomesticated* (winner of Red Flag Poetry's 2020 chapbook contest.)

"Agnes Vojta's poetry is rife with images of nature and the compassion for all living, sentient beings, even the mosquitos that the bats need to eat. It is also a book about loss, as she grapples with her aging parents who live in a continent away, from the home in Germany she left to live in the United States. She compares herself to the starlings that "thrive in their new land," and she visits Dresden, where she finds the maples are the only thing that hasn't changed, as she certainly has in her new home, with a core of being that hasn't. Her book is like the coracle from the title poem, in which her poetry is "large enough to hold a dream/ a dream just light/enough not to sink it." A moving and profound read, Vojta carries us in her coracle to an intimate world, and we are grateful for it."

- Kika Dorsey, author of *Occupied: Vienna is a Broken Man* and *Daughter of Hunger*

A Coracle for Dreams

Poems by Agnes Vojta

Spartan Press
Kansas City, MO
spartanpress.com

Copyright © Agnes Vojta, 2022
First Edition: 1 3 5 7 9 10 8 6 4 2
ISBN: 978-1-952411-94-6
LCCN: 202931277

Cover photos: Agnes Vojta, Penny Thieme
Title photo: Hans Petzold
Author photo: Thomas Vojta
All rights reserved. No part of this publication may be reproduced or transmitted in any form or by any means, electronic or mechanical, including photocopying, recording or by info retrieval system, without prior written permission from the author.

I am grateful to Cortney Collins and Steph Kelln for creating the Zoem poetry community and to Val Szarek and all the other Zoets for filling it with warmth and kindness.

Deep thanks to Aliki Barnstone for her generous encouragement and support.

Thank you, Sophia Vojta, for your thoughtful suggestions that made these poems better. Thanks, KC Dolan and Rachel Schneider, for countless hours of conversations. Thank you, Mimi Hedl, for sharing your garden and your wisdom.

Thank you, Susanne Hampe, for a friendship that helps me stay rooted in the old country. Thank you, Anna Petzold, for taking up the slack back home when I am so far away.

And always, thanks to Thomas Vojta for sharing this journey with me.

I am grateful to the editors of the following publications where some of these poems first appeared, sometimes under a different title:

As it Ought to Be Magazine: "Flotsam", "Vineyard in Dresden", "Love after Fifty Years", "Waiting for News from the Hospital", "Nursing Home Visit in Times of Corona", "Rewired", "I don't Usually Pray"
Bindweed: "Ferrying Turtles", "Shadow", "The One who Left"
Black Coffee Review: "Swallowing Reflex", "Thou Shalt Not Look at a Naked Soul"
Gasconade Review: "Laying Old Ghosts to Rest", "Song for a Hollow Sycamore"
Gyroscope Review: "Status Report"
Hobo Camp Review: "Connected"

Live Nude Poems: "Fall and the Second of Thermodynamics"
Mad Swirl: "Anticipatory Grief"
Made of Rust and Glass: "The Yew Trees with their Bitter Berries", "The Curator"
Muddy River Review: "June Morning at Cook Station", "Today We Burned the Field"
Plants and Poetry: "The Right Place, the Right Time"
San Pedro River Review: "Council Bluff Lake"
Thimble Literary Magazine: "Speechless"
Verse Virtual: "In my Dream", "The Cosmic Bank of Good Deeds"
Young Ravens Literary Review: "Naming"

Table of Contents

Naming / 1

Flotsam / 2

Speechless / 3

First Christmas in Missouri / 4

This Town Does Not Inspire Love Songs / 5

I Do Not Tire of the Miracle of Snow / 6

The One Who Left / 7

Thou Shalt Not Look at a Naked Soul / 8

Laying Old Ghosts to Rest / 10

In My Dream / 12

The Yew Trees with Their Bitter Berries / 13

Birthday Roses / 14

Connected / 15

Involuntary Immigrants / 16

I Hope there Are Mosquitoes / 17

Morning Ritual / 18

Song for a Hollow Sycamore / 19

June Morning at Cook Station / 20

Vineyard in Dresden / 22

Council Bluff Lake / 24

Shadow / 25

Waiting for News from the Hospital / 26

The Patience of the Cicadas / 27

Swallowing Reflex / 28

Rewired / 29

Ferrying Turtles / 30

Status Report / 31

Lectionary / 32

Love, after Fifty Years, / 34

Nursing Home Visit in Times of Corona / 35

Silent Days / 36

The Cosmic Bank of Good Deeds / 37

Today we burned the field / 38

Kin / 40

Time Difference / 41

Creation through Subtraction / 42

Where Do the Memories Go? / 43

The Curator / 44

Gravity Knows no Mercy / 45

Stone Wall in the Ozarks / 46

Inheritance / 48

Anticipatory Grief / 50

Choirs of Stars / 51

A Coracle for Dreams / 52

The Last Picture / 53

May You Go to Your Sleep / 54

The Right Place, the Right Time / 55

Fall and the Second Law of Thermodynamics / 56

I Don't Usually Pray / 57

A Poem Impossible to Title / 58

Eulogy for the Robin I Found on My Patio / 59

Witch Hazel / 60

For my parents,
Hans and Heidi Petzold

*The moment of the rose
and the moment of the yew-tree
Are of equal duration.*

-T. S. Eliot

Naming

My first day here it snowed,
and birds like drops of blood
sat in the grey-green branches of a tree.
I was a stranger. Did not know
the names of tree or birds.

Naming is knowing.
Naming means: to tell apart,
to be familiar with the detail
that separates one from the other.
Familiarity breeds love.

I learned to name the cedars
and the cardinals, anemone
and great blue heron, spiderwort
and wild geranium. Every year,

I add new names: white avens,
thimbleweed, rose-breasted grosbeak –
every one another root
I grow here.

Flotsam

I shipped my past to this continent
in a box I open rarely. In it,

my mother's amber necklace
and my grandmother's silver cross,

a dried carnation from my prom bouquet,
ribboned letters from old lovers,

notebooks with poems written
thirty years ago in another tongue,

a leather pouch I carried around my neck,
a brass key that opens no lock I know,

a photograph of the house on the hill
that stands now empty,

where my voice still echoes, unheard,
five thousand miles away.

Speechless

The mute years are dunes
of unwritten words
that shift with the winds,
memories evanescent as mirages.
I wish I had driven poems
like stakes into the ground
to anchor time.

First Christmas in Missouri

I miss the carols. The boys' choir
singing Bach's Christmas oratorio.

Mom's collection of wooden nutcrackers.
The fat little angels with their green wings.

Christmas pyramids. Herrnhut paper stars.
Mulled wine at the Christkindl market.

I find Lebkuchen at Aldi.
Imported from Germany.

I do not like Lebkuchen
but they smell of cinnamon, anise,

and home. That winter, we are eating
Lebkuchen well into March.

This Town Does Not Inspire Love Songs

Unlike the stately city that was home,
this town does not inspire love songs,

does not enrapture painters, and composers
don't dedicate their symphonies to it.

Eight hundred years of history I traded
for one hundred fifty, cobblestones for asphalt

and sandstone balustrades for clapboard, traded
the opera for the town band where old men

in lederhosen and red knee highs play
on summer Thursdays on the courthouse lawn.

I Do Not Tire of the Miracle of Snow

The streets are empty, the town
a photograph in black and white.
The world slows down
on snow days.

All sounds are muffled,
except for the squeaking
under my feet as I walk
home from work.

Streets, lawns, and roofs
are covered indiscriminately.
The bushes bow low
under their load.

This will not last. The squeaking
will turn to slushing,
and black patches will appear
on the pavement.

Missouri winters teach
about impermanence,
and miracles
don't last.

The One Who Left

Like water flowing downhill,
letters now travel
only in one direction.

Life goes on for those who stayed;
a circle with one person missing
is still a circle.

The one who left floats,
fragile tethers frayed
by the teeth of time and distance.

After some years,
even the Christmas cards
remain unanswered.

Thou Shalt Not Look at a Naked Soul

You sold all your things
before your trip
around the world

hauled them down the stairs
spread them out in the yard,
slices of your life piled high:

books and records
clothes and shoes
a coat rack shaped like a cactus

the tie dye bedspread
the pewter bowl from your windowsill
the necklace with the garnet pendant

your baby pictures
your paintings
your sketch books.

A friend said she wished
she could buy them all and keep
them for you until your return.

I opened one of them,
started to look through the pages
but it felt like a sin.

I could not have
them in my house.
They would whisper

in their box, haunt me—
nobody should own
a piece of another's soul.

Laying Old Ghosts to Rest

Ghosts are heavy.
Carrying them is weary work.

If you try to shake them off,
they grip harder.

But it is time. They too,
have grown tired of you.

You can sing them to sleep
with the right incantation.

Don't sigh or say *if only*.
Don't look backwards.

Dig a grave. Soften
the ground with water, not tears.

Tell them you'll miss them
for a while but you'll be

okay on your own now.
Gently loosen their grip.

Be firm and kind.
Hold their hands for a moment.

Carry them in your arms
with tenderness, like children.

Lay them down softly
and start humming

the happiest song you know.
Cover them with flowers.

In My Dream

I climb the stairs
to the old apartment
I haven't entered
in years.

I get stuck
on the landing below
bricks and boards
block the steps.

The apartment is full
of things I haven't wanted
since I've moved out:
dusty furniture, boxes,

suitcases stuffed
with hand-me-downs.
Mail is still delivered
to the broken letterbox.

I can never reach the door
but I carry the key
in my pocket
and I still pay the rent.

The Yew Trees with Their Bitter Berries

The house sleeps
behind curtains of wine leaves.
The black-and-white tiles
lay crooked and cracked
on overgrown paths.

I see, once a year,
my parents' faces
as in a flip book
that makes time visible
and foreshadows endings.

The garden dozes
in the deep dark green
of rhododendrons
and of the yew trees
with their bitter berries.

Birthday Roses

The childhood roses arched
high on the trellises –
red blossoms,
on my June birthday.
I felt like a princess
in her summer castle.

Rewilded, now
the roses hang
small and pale
on the fallen arches
over cracked stones.

Connected

Your feet are walking
the same earth as mine.
Your eyes look up
at the same sky.
You bare your skin
to the same sun that shines on me.
We are connected
through distance and time.

Perhaps the raindrops
that fall on me
were once part of the creek
in which you swim each day.
Maybe some molecules
of the air I breathe
passed through your lungs
before the wind blew them my way.

And the wild geese
that fly overhead
passed over your house
on their northward journey,
and you heard
their hoarse voices,
and you, too, felt
a strange longing.

Involuntary Immigrants

It is snowing. The bluebirds,
the chickadees, titmice,
and nuthatches
puff up against the cold,
throng the feeders,
peck at suet and sunflower seeds,
desperate for the oily goodness
in this bitter winter.

The starlings, too, plump
their speckled feathers
and descend on the feeders,
greedy for grains and seeds.
I will put out extra;
there is enough for the starlings, too
who are as cold as the bluebirds,
the chickadees, titmice, and nuthatches.

Revered as harbingers of spring
in my homeland, lured
with special bird houses, the starlings
did not ask to be brought
to another continent to be reviled
as non-native invaders,
and that they thrive in their new land–
how can I fault them for that?

I Hope there Are Mosquitoes

The afternoon was warm
but the sunset lures
the cold from its hiding place.
It creeps out from leafless thickets –
a reminder: this is not spring.
Not yet. Even though the cardinals
sing in the cedars, and the robins
pick on the lawns that are soggy
from recent snow melt.

The sky – a watercolor,
pink melting into blue,
the silhouettes of naked trees
etched in black ink.

A tiny bat streaks across the canvas –
too early, little one,
you should still be sleeping,
but for your sake, I hope
there are mosquitoes.

Morning Ritual

I prepare breakfast for my son
who, at seventeen, is perfectly able
to fix his own food. I remember

how dad would wake me up
every morning at six and ask
for my breakfast choice.

The question *"Oats or toast?"*
was our morning ritual.
Throughout high school,

dad made breakfast for me, who,
at seventeen, was perfectly able
to fix her own food. I never

thought much about it. Now I am
doing this small act of love
for my own child.

Song for a Hollow Sycamore

If I come
seeking shelter
you let me in,

open
the charred cell
at your center,

safe
like home
like womb

with a window
to look out
on the world.

You offer me
your presence
without demands,

show me
how to grow
despite gaping wounds.

June Morning at Cook Station

The day is pregnant with heat.
In a few hours, the kids will ride
their bikes to the swim hole,
jump in the water, splash and holler.
Now the only sound is birdsong.

At the General Mercantile,
the *Closed* sign hangs crooked
beside a faded Pepsi poster.
The wooden word *Canoes*
still points toward the river.

On the façade of the bank,
the ornamental brick crumbles.
Paint peels from the frames
of the arch windows.
Weeds have conquered the porch.

Behind the trim white church,
the grass has been cut.
A rosebush blooms by the door.
Under the walnut trees,
a stone bench invites:
sit and rest a while.

Honeysuckle hangs from the fences,
heavy with fragrance.

Spiderwort purples the ditch.
Below the bridge, the water
pools green and cool.

Vineyard in Dresden

The path between the ivied walls
is paved in sandstone. Grass
grows from the cracks. I follow
the trails of childhood.

The cobwebbed door
has not been opened in a long time,
but someone cleared the steps
leading to it. I climb

the stairs into the vineyards,
breathe history, mine and the land's.
Lush and green, the grapes
promise a rich harvest.

Below, the river sings a love song
to the city that is no longer mine.
Eighteen years change
a person and a place.

Not even the trees
are the same; the drought
felled the old oak in the clearing
we called the witches' dance hall.

But the hills and the river
are still there, and dearer

to me than the castles
and cathedrals that lure the tourists.

And the summer light
through the maples remains
unchanged, as all else
grows old and distant.

Council Bluff Lake

The woods drowned
when the dam was built.
We float between cedar ghosts.

Their reflections ripple
black squiggles
in the waves.

A bird flits into a hole
in a dead tree, won't emerge
again while we wait.

The smell of wild roses wafts
over the water. We drift.
Soft air, soft light, soft silence.

Shadow

It is the hour of the bats. They swoop
black across purple sky
between the trees that swallow
the bats into blackness.

My mother and I sit on the porch. Every night
we watch the fireflies appear
and dance on the grass. We cannot
decipher their coded signals.

Mom delights in the fireflies and the bats
and the moon as if she sees them
for the first time. The goodbye
leans its shadow over us. We both know:

this is her last visit. We don't
talk about grave things, only
point out the bats
and drink the last of the wine.

Waiting for News from the Hospital

she is on her knees
scrubbing the kitchen tiles
square by grey square.
The dark lines of grout
meet at right angles.

She erases
a splatter of tomato sauce,
a dusting of flour,
a smear of mud,
scours

until the floor is so clean
she wants to lie down,
cheek to the cool tile,
and breathe
the faint lemon smell.
She wipes her forehead,
stands up and paces
the empty house
looking for something
else to clean.

The Patience of the Cicadas

Seventeen years
buried below,
cradled by roots,
sightless
flightless
soundless
waiting

to heed
a mysterious call
to emerge
from the ground,
to climb into the canopy
of the trees
and to sing
with the whole body.

I have so much to learn
about patience.

Swallowing Reflex

Her father has stopped eating.
Her mother calls;
they must decide
about a feeding tube.

That night, she finds
herself in the grocery store,
filling her cart with cheese,
chocolate, chips,

as if she could eat
for him,
as if she could stuff
the hole

that is opening
in their lives,
threatening
to swallow them.

Rewired

In mom's kitchen, Grandma's
measuring cup is still
on the shelf, her nutmeg grater
hangs from its hook.

For sugar and salt, we still use
the little wooden shovels.
I set the table
with the familiar

blue-and-white dishes,
the placemats my sister
and I weaved that Christmas
we got the looms.

In the pantry, I still reach
for the light switch on the left
where it no longer is.
Dad rewired the kitchen

twenty years ago. I cannot
rewire my brain, cannot train
my hand to reach
to the other side.

Ferrying Turtles

On the logs, the turtles dry in the sun:
cooters, map turtles, sliders.
As I approach, they drop, one by one,
into the river and swim away.

A box turtle is swept along,
bobs up and down, helpless,
wiggles her feet and stretches her neck,
trying to keep her head above water.

I reach her with my paddle,
scoop her up - she slides off with a splash
and floats further. Disappears
under a downed tree.

Reappears, struggling downstream.
I overtake her, grab her by the shell,
plop her into my kayak. Ferry her to the shore,
carry her inland to a patch of grass.

She takes off swiftly. No sign
of hesitation or bewilderment.
Some day she may tell the other turtles
about her encounter with God.

Status Report

I walked along my creek
which is a term of endearment–
one doesn't own a creek any more
than one owns the clouds–

stood on a limestone slab,
watched the ripples on the water,
the reflection of leafless trees,
the darting minnows.

I moved an earthworm
from the path onto the grass.
The robins were eating red berries
off a vine whose name I did not know.

Five crows held council in an oak tree,
flew away when I approached.
Something has been tearing
the Osage oranges to yellow shreds.

I found a purple leaf and a snail shell.
More I did not accomplish –
besides standing, still, in amazement
at the colors of the cardinals.

Lectionary

Open the lectionary
of the forest.
Find chapter and verse
for each season,
each moon cycle.

First full moon
after equinox:
read the maples. Consider
their luminous leaves. Observe
the process of letting go.
Feel it deep in your body.

Listen to the wind
preach his sermon.
Hear the yellow grasses rustle.
They know the secret.
So do the bats.

Go to the river.
She whispers words
that are missing
in the dictionary,
roars them in her rapids.

With enough patience,
you can see the wind

whittle the sandstone.
See autumn slide into winter.
Nobody will solve
the riddle for you.

Perhaps the riddle
has no solution.
Perhaps the puzzle box
cannot be opened.

Love, after Fifty Years,

is an old woman riding the bus
for an hour to a nursing home.
Her husband does not speak.
She does not have much

to say, but today his fingers
closed around her hand.
She stays until the end
of the allowed time.

She will have just missed
the bus. She wanders
the deserted cobblestone streets
of the small town.

Most shops closed at five.
A bakery is still open. She buys
a cookie to eat on the way.
It is autumn, the dusk falls early.

She rides home through the dark.
When she steps into her empty
house, she hopes she will
get to do this again soon.

Nursing Home Visit in Times of Corona

You must make an appointment by phone.
You must call between ten and three on a weekday.
You may only visit once a week.
You must visit between 1 and 5 pm.
You may not stay longer than one hour.
You must check in fifteen minutes before.

You must fill out a form.
You must wear a face mask.
You must keep a distance.
You must disinfect your hands.
You must walk to the building along the shortest way
you have been directed to use.

You must check in with the nurse.
You must wait if the nurse is busy.
You may not speak with a doctor.
You must make an appointment to call the doctor
by phone if you have questions.
You must check out with the nurse.

You receive a check mark by your name.
You get a green mark if you kept the time limit.
You get a red mark if you overstayed.
If you have a red mark,
you may be denied
further visits.

Silent Days

She collects the words
that dribble from her husband's lips,

a spoon full each day, to water
her parched life. She soaks

them up to sustain her
through the monotony of nursing.

Some days, he gives her an entire sentence.
Some days, only a shake of head – perhaps

he does not feel there is anything left
to say, or nothing that justifies the effort.

Sometimes she still glimpses
his sense of humor in a phrase.

Those days feel lighter
and less lonely.

The Cosmic Bank of Good Deeds

My mother's garden
lies untended.
I send her flowers
over the internet. My hands

help another woman
on a different continent
mow her grass,
plant her tomatoes –

small deposits
into the cosmic bank
of good deeds. I hope
mom can make a withdrawal.

Today we burned the field

It started small:
one match,
three orange tongues
that licked the yellow grass.

The fire grew,
ate through the dried
stems of last year's
asters and coneflowers,
devoured
leaves, nibbled
at the indigo bush –

a hungry beast
that roared and reared up
when it reached
the switchgrass,
made us shrink
back from its fury.

A breeze awoke
and drove the flames
towards the neighbor's pasture.
We raced to beat them
into submission
with heavy shovels.

Later, the last twigs
curled in the ashes.
Here and there
nests of smoke
still smoldered.

And high above,
flocks of snow geese traveled
northward. We heard
their cries before our eyes
could find them.

Kin

I take pictures of birds,
email them to my mother.
She recognizes
the Carolina wren, cousin
to the Eurasian wren
they call *Zaunkönig,*
king-of-the-fence,
funny name for such a tiny thing.

The blue jays and chickadees
have cousins in Germany, too:
Eichelhäher and *Meise.*
I no longer
have cousins in Germany.

No bird there resembles
the cardinal. Mom remembers
cardinals from her visits.
She shows the pictures to dad.
We do not know
if he understands
what they are.

Time Difference

At lunch, I call my mother
before the evening nurse
comes to ready dad
for the night.

I sit in sunshine. High
above, a hawk soars.
My day just passed
its zenith.

My mother's day
is almost spent.
Soon shadows descend,
usher in the darkness.

Creation through Subtraction

In the *Economist*,
I read about the cells in the leaves,
the mesophylls that capture
sunlight and air, wisely arranged

veins run through the tree,
the xylem draws water
up from the roots;
the phloem sends sugars
to the tips of the furthest branches.

Come, marvel at the patterns,
the miraculous order:
how following the rules of physics
creates a living being.

I sit by the river
watch the leaves
quiver in the wind,
murmur as if in prayer.
The spirit understands
the archaic language.

Between greening and letting go,
the trees put on a show
as chlorophyll breaks down, leaves
the other colors visible.
Creation through subtraction.

Where Do the Memories Go?

I asked dad to write down
his childhood memories,
the story of my grandparents,
how he met mom.

He bought a dictation machine
he could never get to work.
He started typing, read me
the first page, lost the draft.

Too late to begin again.
The memories are imprisoned
behind his brow.
A life sentence.

If they are still
in there. Perhaps
they have shriveled
like the spiderwort flowers

that bloom one morning
and dissolve into purple liquid,
enclosed by the sepals
like a brain enclosed by a skull.

The Curator

Deserted, the museum dozes. Artifacts lie forlorn in their glass cases. Their labels peel, curl, the glue consumed by tiny bugs. Helmets and armor, a sword with a broken hilt. Ceramic shards. Beads that once were a necklace. Books in a font only scholars can now decipher. Ancient garments, moth-eaten.

The historic maps in their frames show countries that have descended into obsolescence: borders dissolved; civilizations crumbled like the pressed flowers on the display cards in the natural history section. Stuffed birds sit mounted on branches; the beady eyes lost their sheen and the feathers their colors.

The curator walks from room to room. The wooden floor creaks under his halting steps. He does not remember when he came here. He unlocks the building each morning, gets out the metal cash box with the tickets and the change. He does not wait for visitors anymore.

The world has forgotten the museum. Perhaps it no longer needs the past. The curator does. He is on intimate terms with his exhibits. Could answer any question about the countries or the armor. Could name the birds. If anyone were asking.

He is the memory keeper, the sage who could tell you the legends before they sink into the mist of myth. He walks his round and recites the guided tour narrative to himself so he won't forget.

Gravity Knows no Mercy

The vine clings
to the house,
its tendrils claw
the mortar, burrow
in the masonry.

The wind stole
shingles off the roof
and bent
the weathervane.

The stone wall in the back
is crumbling.
There is no mason now
who can repair it.

The mountain presses,
a relentless mass
of soil and trees
that slowly slides.

Stone Wall in the Ozarks

Dream-driven, they came
from the East, settled

by the creek
in a valley of promise.

Patient hands piled
river rocks, marked

the homestead –
a testament to hope.

The land shriveled the hope.
Broke the promise.

Briars conquered
the pasture. Shrubs

swallowed the garden,
vines the barn.

Inside the farmhouse
wallpaper scraps,

a broken shelf, the shards
of pink porcelain cups.

The wall remains.
Trees grow in the gaps.

The low sun slants
a last beam over the stones.

The sweetgum leaves
are fallen stars.

Inheritance

To remember my grandma,
I asked for the mushroom painting
that hung in her drawing room:
chanterelles and boletes

piled on the wooden table,
bursting out of the frame.
A stoneware jug heaped
with blackberries.

Dad wanted to keep
it, said I would inherit
it. He did not say
when I die.

When I was six, he taught me
to find redcaps under the birches,
chanterelles by the side
of the paths under the pines.

He showed me the bay boletes
with their brown velvet caps,
how to press their spongy underside,
wait for the telltale blue.

I marched home proudly
with our finds. Dad despised
the taste, could not stand
the smell of mushrooms.

My mother likes them.
Now she can cook them
whenever she wants.
It feels like a betrayal.

Anticipatory Grief

You have learned
there is a word
for this

mourning someone
who is not yet
dead

liminal space
between hope
and letting go

lingering
at the threshold
of loss

no-man's land
you must cross
on your own

afraid
to reach
the other side

Choirs of Stars

The creek is a mirror. I wake in darkness, before the moonrise, see lights glimmering around me like the eyes of nocturnal creatures: the reflections of stars on the still water. Choirs of stars sing above me, frequencies beyond human hearing. If we could sleep under these stars each night, healing might be possible.

In my house, the cat curls up in her basket. She comes inside now that the nights are cool. This may be her last summer. She still eats. She moves slowly and does not wander far anymore. Mostly she sleeps.

In my childhood home on the other side of the ocean, my father lies in his bed. For his birthday, I send him flowers. They will cheer up my mother. My mother bakes a cake he will not eat. Dad mostly sleeps.

Autumn will soon gild the leaves. The swallows have left their nests in the cliffs, pilot their way south. Seeds fall and lay themselves to sleep in the soil. They need to lie through a cold winter so they can germinate. Maybe there's a metaphor in that.

A Coracle for Dreams

On the way to the river,
we pass the tie dye shop.
Swirls and spirals
twist on the fabric.
I am a hippie at heart.

We listen to Neil Young.
It takes me back to Oregon
where Decade was our only tape.
We played it on all the drives
up the McKenzie pass road.
Mountains and life
seemed limitless then.

I watch a leaf sail
through the air, land
on the water, float
away like a little boat.
A coracle just large
enough to hold a dream,
a dream just light
enough not to sink it.

The Last Picture

The house sighs.
It has heard it before:
how the stairs creak
under halting steps,
more slowly each day.

With dusty eyes, it looks out
on the leaf strewn patio.
The pathway between the hedges
has grown narrow.

The house remembers laughter
giving way to hushed voices,
rooms that feel heavy with sadness.

After a long silence,
the bustle of strange feet,
then emptiness.

On the wall
a faded rectangle remains,
shadow of a green landscape.

May You Go to Your Sleep

May you go to your sleep
like a boat unmoored,
quietly gliding
free from the shore.

May you float away
carried by currents
cradled by waves
that rock you gently.

May you suffer no storm,
no shouting crew,
no helmsman fighting
to alter your course.

May you calmly drift
through peaceful waters
to the green country
beyond the horizon.

The Right Place, the Right Time

The river has no regrets.
She does not wish herself back
to the hills where she was born,
to the bluffs she once passed.

The river does not make plans.
She does not rush somewhere
that is not here, does not yearn
for distant meadows.

The river does not want
to be anything but a river—
every drop in the right place
at the right time,

and every place is the right place,
every time the right time.

Fall and the Second Law of Thermodynamics

It is the season of apples, crisp and tart. I transform them into crumbles, pies, and comfort. They soften, lose their texture, sink into sugary union with the flour.

September lifts the hazy skies of Missouri summer. Contours become clearer. The woods fill with yellow wildflowers, the species easy to confuse.

Confusion is easier than clarity. The second law of thermodynamics requires nature to fall from order into disorder. Atomic arrangements disintegrate. Ink dropped into a glass of water disperses, forms a cloud, spreads until the liquid is pale blue. Bubbles burst, unable to sustain surface tension. Organisms die.

Autumn is the season of disordering. Of decay. Leaves fall; highly organized matter turns to soil. Re-turns to soil. Death is but an increase in entropy. If you look at it like that, there is nothing to fear.

I Don't Usually Pray

My father is still alive
when I switch off the phone,
board the plane.
My mother pleads
with him: hang on, wait,
just one more night.

I ask for a glass of wine.
I don't usually drink.
Today I hope it dulls
the edge of grief,
lulls me to forget
where I travel.

Over the Atlantic,
I dissolve in weeping.
I don't usually cry.
The flight attendant asks
if she can do anything.
Make the plane fly faster.

I keep checking
the flight status,
I will search my sister's face
when she picks me up.
I don't usually pray.
I pray to be in time.

A Poem Impossible to Title

The day after my mother's birthday, the telephone keeps ringing. Mom thanks the callers for their well-wishes. When they ask how she is doing, she tells them her husband passed away that morning. Shocked silence. Tears. Mumbled words of sympathy.

All day, the sky is like glass, the air transparent. The sun is setting when they carry my father down the stairs.

We extinguish the candles. Leave the vase with the white flowers, the mirror shrouded in a linen sheet. Through the open window, cold air creeps into the room, into our bones.

My mother believes in God. I do not. But when I look up at the milky way, I have a sensation of eternity.

Eulogy for the Robin I Found on My Patio

Thank you for letting me hold you,
little feathery miracle. You were huddled
on the frozen ground, head tucked under,
as if you were going to sleep.

I picked you up, gently, carried
you into the warmth, marveled
at the orange feathers on your breast,
the intricate pattern of your wings.

I am sorry I found you too late –
you will not sing in the spring.
It seems silly to cry over a bird
but every drop of love

flows back to the love
that pulses the universe,
and even compassion
for a dead robin is not wasted.

Witch Hazel

I have not written
in a long time,
there's too much to say,
and I do not know
where to begin.

Let me just tell you
what I did today.
I fed the cat, sat
with my coffee cup,
watched the sun rise.

I went to the woods.
It was cold. I found
frost flowers at noon
under the deep blue
Ozark winter sky.

I walked by the creek
to the old mill, little
more than a shack.
The water rushed
down red rhyolite rocks,

and the witch hazel
have started to bloom.
They smell so lovely.
I hope they are blooming
where you are, too.

Agnes Vojta grew up in Germany, spent a few years in California, Oregon, and England, and now lives in Rolla, Missouri where she teaches physics at Missouri S&T and hikes the Ozarks. She is the author of *Porous Land* (Spartan Press, 2019) and *The Eden of Perhaps* (Spartan Press, 2020), and her poems have appeared in a variety of magazines. Her website is agnesvojta.com.

www.ingramcontent.com/pod-product-compliance
Lightning Source LLC
Chambersburg PA
CBHW030350100526
44592CB00010B/903